# Coloring Book for Stress Relieving Designs for Adults Relaxation
# Clever Fox

# This ColoringBook Is Belongs To

__________________________________________

__________________________________________

__________________________________________

9 789858 924431